GUIDED BY THE HOLY SPIRIT

I0624013

IF MY PEOPLE WHO ARE CALLED BY MY NAME

2 CHRONICLES: 7:14

ISBN:978-1-988785-09-7

PUBLISHER

Envision Urban

info@envisionurban.com

Dedication

This story is dedicated to my mother, who came to Florida on vacation and became ill. She then went on to be with the Lord while on vacation. I know she is still on vacation. She is spending it with our heavenly Father.

My mother was an entrepreneur before the word became popular.

She made ladies' undergarments, hats, children's clothing, and pastries to sell. This is how she supported her family.

She then immigrated from Guyana to America in 1973, took a course in childcare, and started her own business. She provided holistic care for children when their parents were on their respective jobs. She retired in good health when she was eighty years old.

*I thank **God** for gifting me with a mother like her. Her favorite saying was "**But God.**" My mom lived her life like someone who knew that **God** had the final say.*

Table of Contents

Chapter One: My Testimony of Hearing *God*'s Voice   **1**

Chapter Two: Learning to Trust *God*   **3**

Chapter Three: Learning to Obey the Guidance of the Holy Spirit   **9**

Chapter Four- *God* Wants His Children to be Obedient   **27**

Chapter Five- Fasting, Praying, Singing   **34**

Chapter Six- Therefore, I Walk in *God*'s Love and Light   **42**

Chapter Seven- *God* is Speaking. Are You Listening?   **47**

CHAPTER ONE

MY TESTIMONY OF HEARING
GOD'S VOICE

"

*I am made in the image and after the likeness of **God**, through Jesus Christ, therefore I am a spiritual being.*

Genesis 1:26

June 1968 is significant for me on a variety of levels. It began when I left Georgetown, Guyana, (formerly British Guyana) on a nine-seat plane and flew to Trinidad, where I boarded a ship for Paris, France, the following day.

Both flying and sailing were new to me. The trip to France lasted for fourteen ecstatic

1

days. I was then supposed to travel by train to Essex, England, to pursue studies in nursing. I later realized that *God* had other plans for my life. Just as I was about to board the train heading to England, I discovered I did not have the necessary travel documents to land in England. I was so disappointed and saddened that my passport was not officially stamped and valid.

As a result, I needed to return to Guyana. Looking back at this experience, I felt like a sailor because I spent fourteen more days on the ship for my return journey. At that point, I didn't know where or how things would turn out. What I learned through that experience, though, was that I had to allow *God* to take the lead in my life. In essence, I was learning the importance of trusting *God*.

But God

CHAPTER TWO

LEARNING TO TRUST *GOD*

"

*For who hath known the mind of the
Lord, that he may instruct him? But we
have the mind of Christ
1 Corinthians 2:16*

Because I have the mind of Jesus Christ, I
now have the wisdom, knowledge, and
understanding to make good decisions.

One night, as I was sleeping on the ship back
to Guyana, I had a ***Joseph-like dream
experience***. It is a dream that I still clearly
remember. There was an elderly woman who
looked as if she was in her late eighties or
nineties. She had a full head of white hair. I
did not recognize her as someone I knew.

However, she told me to say the words *Jehovah Jireh. Jehovah Jireh*! This was the first time I heard the term. At that time, the term was like a foreign language to me.

I did not know what it meant. Yet, coming from an older person who seemed as if she was full of wisdom, I started to repeat "*Jehovah Jireh"* until it sank into my being.

Later, as I reflected on that experience, I felt it was guidance from *God*, primarily because it came at a time of deep disappointment at having to give up my plans to study nursing. Frequently, I would say *Jehovah Jireh* Genesis 22:14, which means "*God* will provide." It's funny how I associated this woman's gray hair with wisdom.

The culture I grew up in would share many proverbs with the younger generations. Much like today, these wise sayings were meant to help us navigate our way through the world.

The one proverb that still resonates with me states: *"Pig ask im Mumma wha mek har mout' long so? Mumma sey, no mind pickney, yuh a grow, yuh wi see."* In other words, the mother pig was telling her piglet that as he gets older, he will learn that he needs a longer mouth to dig for his food. As I grew older, I eventually realized that most elderly people are blessed with wisdom. I now know that age and experience can lead to knowledge, wisdom, and a heightened sense of insight.

Weeks before my travel date was set, I went to the British Embassy to apply for a visa to England. The officer at the Embassy interviewed me. He took my passport; I heard him stamp it - or so I thought. I then walked away, convinced that I had been issued a visa. Yet it was not until I arrived in France that I saw there was no visa or stamp on my passport.

The vicissitudes of life taught me that I had a lot of growing up to do. I should have checked my passport before leaving the Embassy.

I am the fifth child in my family, and having three older sisters, I always looked for or expected encouragement and guidance from an older sibling in whatever situation or task was ahead of me.

Even though our mother was present, we tended to mentor and coach each other. I was slowly beginning to learn not to put my trust in family members but instead to trust *God* Almighty. Jeremiah 1:5 says, "*Before I was formed in my mother's belly God knew me.*"

Growing up in a mother-led household with seven other siblings, I was taught by my mother to pray to my only Father, who is in Heaven. I said both the 23rd and 91st Psalms regularly. These psalms spoke of **God** being my provider and my protector.

In August of that same year, when I returned to Guyana, an older sister studying to become a beautician in America sent me an application form for a school in New York. I applied to that school and was accepted. By December 13, 1968, I was in America, preparing to start classes in January. Wow! What an exciting and liberating feeling.

Of course, it was so long ago that I do not recall the cost of the plane ticket. Nevertheless, I was able to purchase it because family members and friends chipped in. Some gave sixty dollars, some fifty, some thirty. I hope I paid them all back. At least, I think I did.

I was indeed grateful that *God* had provided a way for me to leave Guyana in search of an education and, ultimately, a better lifestyle.

In retrospect, I know that my passion to seek an education in nursing was certainly not *God*'s plan for my life. I know for a fact now that *God* does not make mistakes.

"God Can Do Exceedingly Abundantly Above All That We Ask or Think. Ephesians 3:20."

But God

Chapter Three

GUIDANCE OF THE HOLY SPIRIT

"

*When my obedience is fulfilled, **God** will avenge all disobedience.*

2 Corinthians 10:6

I met my husband in Guyana when I was eighteen years old. One year later, he joined me in New York. We made our relationship official in 1970, with a wedding when I was 22.

In re-examining our courtship, I cannot remember experiencing butterflies as shown in the movies or what is written in romance novels. Nor did I feel he was the person I would be with for the rest of my life.

9

One of the first things he told me about himself was that he sang in a church choir. I had noticed that when he sang, his voice sounded like a choir. Indeed, he sings well. Naivety led me to believe that because he sang in the church choir, he was a *God-fearing man.*

He has always been loving, attentive, and respectful to me. It also seemed as if he would give me the world if he could. For those reasons, I grew to love and trust him.

When we were youngsters, people were not encouraged to express thoughts and feelings. I believe that this had a great impact on the way we learned to communicate. Because of his communication style and because of my desire or need to avoid conflict at all costs, I overlooked situations that should have been discussed. My only goal was to keep the peace between us.

On reflection, my communication style during my early years of marriage could be considered passive by Western standards. I had many lessons to learn about myself and intimate relationships. As I grew older and closer to *God*, it eventually dawned on me that *God* was using all my life experiences to refine and draw me closer to Him. He knows and sees all, but I needed to be quiet to hear what *God* wanted me to hear.

Something very significant happened one evening when I was walking home from Bible study. I heard a thundering Voice say, "*And we shall live together forever and ever.*" I knew *God* was trying to get my attention. This is a good time to pause and declare that *God* speaks to each of us in different ways. What is important is that He talks to His children. He spoke to Balaam through a donkey.
Numbers 22:21-30.

On another occasion, I was driving home from work on a Friday afternoon. It was raining heavily. While I was trying to keep safe during the torrential downpour, I heard a loud Voice that said, ***"If you do not stop eating how you are eating."***

"Eating?" I thought. As I paused to consider and think seriously about the statement, I had to admit that I was indeed over-gorging myself with whatever was in sight.

Upon more reflection, I realized that my quantities and quality were not healthy by any stretch of the imagination. I did not doubt that I was hearing from my Heavenly Father - and I wanted to be obedient. So, I became more aware and intentional about my eating habits. I was reminded that my body is ***God's temple.*** I needed to be led by the ***Holy Spirit***, as stated in Matthew 4:4.

It had always been my dream to own my home. My husband and I lived in an apartment for over 20 years. Whenever I attempted to discuss purchasing a house with my partner, he was not in the least interested.

He was not the type to hammer nails and be handy around the house - no painting walls or cutting grass for him. I learned not to argue, convince, or try to persuade. I knew that **God** was my defender. I prayed and left it in **God**'s hands.

One day, I heard a Voice say, "**LEAVE!**"
I ignored that Voice. I knew **God** would not tell me to leave my marriage and my home. Then I heard it again. But this time, the Voice said, "**LEAVE NOW!**" As would be expected, I was startled.

By now, I had grown accustomed to hearing from the **Holy Spirit,** *so* I trusted the Voice. I obeyed what I believed to be the Voice of the **Holy Spirit** and did not return home from work that day. In obedience, I had to submit my will to **God**. I left with the clothes on my back. Without any effort on my part, we moved into our first house three months later. My only involvement in the arrangement was to obey and trust the **Holy Spirit**.

Suffice it to say, my husband became the best renovator and handy person in the family. He has now replaced the wood floor in the entire house. He became the resident electrician. He was now painting and doing a wide variety of tasks around the house. **God is good!** My dearly beloved, who never attended trade school or cooking classes, cooks like a pro and enjoys all those survival activities. **God is good, and God is great**! He does things in His way and in His time.

As many of us are aware, Florida is known for its hurricanes. We now live in Florida. A few years ago, we experienced a raging hurricane that destroyed everything in its path. We lost shingles from our roof that would have cost thousands to replace. Instead, my husband addressed the roof problem for twenty-eight dollars. That was a miracle to me. Not only has *God* been working on me, but He has my husband in His hands, and as the hymn goes, "Under His Wings."

I am reminded that when we believe that *God* is in charge and make every effort to be obedient, *God* will use whoever He wants to do His will in our lives.

Throughout this book, I have shared my experiences hearing *God's* Voice. But allow me to start from the beginning again.

It all started in the 1980s. I had some cash that I wanted to donate to a church. However, I was not a churchgoer at that time. Sitting on my bed one morning, I heard a Voice say, "**Send it to Gene Profeta.**" I was puzzled. I had never heard the name before. I wondered, *"who on earth is Gene Profeta?"*

About six months later, I was conversing with a young woman who worked in the same building as me. We were sharing about the goodness of *God* in our lives, and I asked her if she had ever heard the name Gene Profeta.

"Yes, he is the pastor of a church in Long Island," she replied. I researched, found his contact information via the telephone company's operator, and sent my gift. I am eternally grateful that *God* is shepherding me, as He promised in Psalms 23: "**The Lord is my shepherd. I shall not want.**"

When I reflect on my life, I realize that I am indeed being guided by the *Spirit of Jesus Christ.*

For a short period, I was unemployed. I did not attend church on a consistent basis. But I fasted and prayed regularly. There were times when I prayed at six, nine, twelve, three, and six again. Over the Lenten season, I would pray and try to observe a true Lent by fasting for forty days. This taught me to discipline myself.

At one point, I was seeking *God* for guidance and direction regarding car ownership. I was not courageous enough to go car shopping on my own at that time.

While sitting on my bed one day, I heard a Voice saying, "*And you have the money*." At that time, I had six thousand dollars stashed away. I could afford to get a car. Nevertheless, it took three months for my husband to agree that I needed my own vehicle so I would not have to depend on him to chauffeur me. According to 1 Corinthians 1:5, "*We are enriched by Him in everything*." *God* was enriching my life with a car in 1987.

In the beginning, hearing voices was not a warm, comforting feeling, especially when no one else was around. It can be particularly frightening. When I started hearing the Voice of the *Holy Spirit*, I was afraid and decided to seek counsel. It was all confusing. I tried, with my human experience and minuscule knowledge, to understand what was happening.

My first appointment was with a priest from Our Lady of Refuge, the Catholic Church on Ocean Avenue in New York. I asked the priest what was happening to me.

"Am I possessed?" I asked. His response made me smile, but it was comforting. He said, "The devil does not need you."

Then I spoke to a Pentecostal minister, and she told me to keep praying. The third person I spoke with was Ms. Lynch, who was at the time a minister from the Unity Church of Christianity. She assured me that I was still sane and healthy. Even though I did not fully comprehend, I was aware that my experiences or challenges were making me stronger and stronger in my faith.

One Saturday evening, I was on the floor of my house praying and crying out to *God*, and I heard the Voice say, "*Do not cry. You need your strength to fight against the forces of darkness.*" That is when I realized that my crying was making me weak. Suddenly, the power of Ephesians 6:12 became clear to me.

"for we wrestle not against flesh and blood, but against principalities, against powers, against the rulers of the darkness of this world, against spiritual wickedness in high places."

Many years ago, I was waiting for my hairdresser's appointment when I overheard a conversation about a young man who regularly heard voices. I was told, eventually, he was diagnosed with a mental illness.

Another story I heard was about a young woman I knew who heard voices coming from the electrical outlet in her home. Of course, this woman is much older now.

Today, despite the so-called voices that she heard, she has successfully raised four children and has several grandchildren and great-grandchildren. She seems to be quite normal to me. I may not understand many things, but I do know my Bible tells me that I should cast all my cares on *God*, and He will direct my path. 1 Peter 5:7.

I have learned that whenever a situation seems hopeless, I will not try to figure it out but will give it to *God*. There are many things that we cannot fathom. One thing I am confident and feel blessed about is that I live my life according to the Bible verse, Proverbs 3:5, which reminds us not to lean on our own understanding.

Daily, I pray to *God* to strengthen my belief and faith.

One Sunday evening, I was in bed next to my husband while he was watching television. I believe that the *Holy Spirit* led me to recite the ninety-first Psalm. I closed my eyes to focus on what I was saying. At that moment, I saw what appeared to be two angels fluttering as they hovered over the foot of my bed. I must admit, it was a scary experience. I tried to call out to my husband twice, but no words would come out. My lips were sealed like a locked door. This experience especially spoke to me. I believe it was a message from the *Spirit of God,* telling me that some things should not be voiced. There is room for reflection and silence.

I continue to believe and know that *God* is good and allows *His Spirit* to speak to and through me. Again, I feel strongly that everyone may not experience what I have and continue to as I walk with *God*.

Another profound spiritual experience occurred when I worked in a physician's office. The owner's partner sat in the office working through a puzzle in the New York Times. Surprisingly, this doctor turned to me and asked if there was a book in the Bible called Habakkuk. I did not think long enough but quickly responded, "No." I considered myself a water-baptized and Spirit-filled believer who had read the Bible many times over. Yet, I didn't remember. As soon as I got home from work, I checked. When I saw it, I thought that if I wanted to share the word and love of **God** with others, then I needed to ask for wisdom and knowledge from the Lord. This was a very humbling lesson for me.

That experience taught me the importance of asking **God** for answers and humility. I am fully aware now that there is so much to learn about myself from the Word of **God**.

I am also beginning to understand Isaiah 28:9 - 10, which tells us, "***Knowledge comes from precept upon precept.***" In other words, it took many individuals, groups, and experiences to contribute to my spiritual growth.

My cousin Desiree would encourage me to fast and pray whenever I was dealing with a valley situation. My older sister would tell me to do everything in and with love. My younger sister would listen to my grumbling and murmurs. I was constantly reminded of a statement made by a TV preacher, John Hagee, who invited his listeners to send their emotions to school.

With that in mind, I recalled a situation I experienced with a young woman I met in college. She had been invited to a job interview. She stopped at my home for a brief visit on her way to the interview. I asked her if she wanted me to pray for her success. She agreed, and I started to pray that *God* would grant her favor so that she would be offered the position. I was wearing slippers, and the floor we were on was fully carpeted. As I prayed, I heard a loud Voice say, "*Take off your shoes; where you stand is Holy ground.*" Exodus 3:5. **God** blessed this young woman by giving her the job. She became very successful and was able to provide for her three children. Her experience assured me that **God** is good and great and that we need to lean on His arm and strength.

But God

CHAPTER FOUR

GOD WANTS HIS CHILDREN TO BE OBEDIENT

"

To obey is better than sacrifice.

1 Samuel 15:22

Over the years, I have developed a passion for reading. My preference is self-enhancement books. I was feeding my spiritual and emotional voids with books. As soon as I finished one, I started another. I found most of the books I read relaxing and soothing. As I grew in Christ, my thirst and hunger for the written word have never changed. One of the first books I read was Wayne "**Dyer's *Your Erroneous Zones***" Another book that contributed to my growth is

Mary Kay's *"You Can Have It All!"* Mary Kay encourages readers to organize and live a disciplined life. She suggests sorting mail as soon as they arrive. She goes on to explain the ills of procrastinating. This, along with many other books I read, helped me become more organized in my thoughts and actions.

Since reading brought such joy and peace to my life, I continue to do it as one of my joy-giving activities. I believe that books are helping me to send my emotions to school.

I also benefited from Deepak Chopra and Charles Capps' written words. Charles Capps *The Tongue* taught me how to speak positive words to myself. Of course, there were times when I could not afford to purchase books. I would then borrow from the library. If the library did not have it on the shelf, I would place a hold on the titles until they were available. Sometimes, I had to wait as long as two weeks to get a particular book I requested.

As I read book after book, I became serene and experienced great peace I never knew. I began telling others to make it a blessed day. I believe that people could speak peace and joy into their lives and the lives of others.

I believe very firmly that the Spirit of **God** is speaking to His children as is explained in Isaiah 30:21: ***"And thine ears shall hear a word behind thee, saying, this is the way, walk ye in it, when ye turn to the right hand, or when ye turn to the left***." **God** does not show favoritism. All He needs is for His children to be obedient.

One of my younger sisters teaches her children that obedience is far better than sacrifice. I heard this over and over. Obedience means to follow and live life as the

Bible teaches. **God** did not reveal His blessings to me until I became obedient.

In Deuteronomy 31:6, **God** promises He will never leave or forsake us. I understood this to mean that He is always guiding, protecting, teaching, and taking care of me. All I must do is acknowledge that **God**'s holy angels have charge over me. He is the same yesterday, today, and forever. He spoke to Moses through the burning bush in Exodus 3:1-17. I know for sure that He is still speaking to His children today.

All **God**'s children have the guidance of the **Spirit of Jesus Christ**. All that is needed is to learn to listen and obey. John 10:27 says, "**My sheep hear My Voice, and I know them, and they follow Me**."

As we walk and grow in Christ Jesus, we are guided and stretched out of our comfort zone. This is how we grow spiritually.

I know that as Christians, we pray and expect **God** to answer our prayers. He invites our prayers, and He is faithful in answering, even if the answer is not what we expect.

I started writing about my relationship with **God** after many years of putting off telling my story. After all, I am neither a preacher nor a writer. I kept asking myself, "***What could I have to offer a reader? Why me?***" I know that **God** uses whom He pleases to do His will. **God** does not have physical hands. He needs His children to do His will. I am learning and growing in grace and understanding as I see my life become richer and fuller. I now understand that **God** qualified me by giving me these experiences to encourage believers to become stronger in their faith. And for non-believers to understand the goodness of *God*. Both believers and non-believers will have a testimony. I am now convinced that I am hiding my testimony under a bushel if I do not share.

I have learned to put on the whole armor of *God* to stand against the schemes of the enemy, as it says in Ephesians 6:11.

If I can help one person whose relationship with *God* is nonexistent or vague to know that *God* wants us to trust Him in all of life's challenges, then I know that my living will not be in vain. Our Father answers prayers in the morning, at noontime, and evening. He stays with his children on the mountain and in the valley.

My understanding of Hebrews 13:8 is that Jesus Christ is the same yesterday, today, and forever. This tells me that **God** does not change. Isaiah 55:3 says, "*If I Trust God, He will make an everlasting covenant with me.*" As **God** leads me onward in my growing awareness and spiritual unfolding, I feel peaceful and content in knowing I will experience more of His goodness on the path set before me.

But God

CHAPTER FIVE

FASTING, PRAYING, SINGING

"

This kind cannot come out without

fasting and praying.

Mark 9:29

Much like my cousin Dcsircc coached me, the church I attended encouraged members to fast. As I began a twenty-one-day fast, I started studying Revelation 5:2. This scripture came alive to me, particularly when I read about John's experience. He wrote: **"*I saw a strange angel proclaiming with a loud voice*"** just as I heard a thundering Voice as I was walking home from a Bible class in New York one evening. My life experiences with **God** and the **Holy Spirit** tells me that fasting and praying are necessary practices for *God* to give guidance. By fasting and praying, we are looking to *God* for solutions to life's situations or problems. There is no doubt that He strengthens us along life's journey as we grow spiritually.

As a constant reminder of the goodness of *God*, I would sing the old hymn written by Civilla Durfee Martin: *"God will take care of me, through every day, o'er all the way." When I wasn't singing that song, I was singing Jesus, Jesus, Jesus! There is something about that Name."* At a point in my life, I knew with certainty that *God* was taking care of me even when I asked for nothing. My *God* was supplying all my needs according to His riches in glory Philippians 4:19.

Some years ago, at the Christian Cultural Center in Brooklyn, Pastor A.R. Bernard preached about Ephesians 3:20. This passage reminds us that **God** is able to do exceedingly abundantly above all we could ask or think.

Of course, the significance of this promise took me a while to internalize and apply to my life. I know now that if I obey **God**'s words and trust Him, all will be well in my life. It is not that we would not have to experience challenges. Having lived this long, I know that challenges will present themselves. We live in a complex world ridden with individual and collective trials. All I know is that these challenges make us stronger. I promise you that life's battles will make us spiritually mature.

Consistently in this story, I have mentioned my weaknesses and tests. One happened when I was younger and had less experience. I was in college and needed to give a presentation to the class. As I stood and began the presentation, I could feel my legs shaking. The bottom of my white skirt was shaking. I was nervous about public speaking.

Years later, I was asked to read a few verses in a Bible study class. All participants were expected to read. I declined because of fear and nervousness. Just a few weeks later, I was asked to make a presentation at the church I attended. I did, and it went well.

Numerous reports speak about the fear of public speaking. **"In *The Vote of Confidence*,** by Nicola Martin," she suggests that public speaking regularly ranks as the nation's biggest fear. It is said to be one of the most prevalent fears in the world.

I am delighted to announce that I was able to overcome my fear of public speaking by drawing on and grounding myself in the scripture Philippians 4:13, which declares, "*I can do all things through Christ who strengthens me.*"

As a mother who believed strongly in the power of speaking positive words to children, I would teach my daughter never to allow anyone to tell her that she was not capable of accomplishing anything, even if they were saying it in jest. As an adult overseeing her own life, she made a choice that I thought was an unwise choice. I asked her what guided her decision as I was admonishing her for the choice she had made. At that moment, I forgot what I had taught her. In keeping with my belief and godly mindset, I asked the *Holy Spirit* if I erred in saying what I said to her. The *Spirit* reminded me that I am reprimanded when I err.

For the first time, my eyes were then opened to *God*'s correction in my life. Just knowing that *God* gives us the strength to accomplish what He wants us to do, regardless of our perceived limitations, is truly amazingly reassuring and comforting.

I am reminded of Judges 6:12, which states: "**When the angel of the Lord appeared to Gideon, he said, The Lord is with you mighty warrior.**" If we believe and accept the Word of **God**, we could claim that we are mighty warriors against our challenges and foes.

Another vivid experience of **God**'s guidance in my life happened in 2007. I worked for the Department of Health in the school system at that time. I was led to work during the summer program. In July, I was sitting in a classroom at my desk while my supervisor was sitting at another desk beside me. I distinctly heard a Voice say, "**Start saving for a house.**" Because I had reaped the benefits of obedience previously, I started to save vigorously. One year later I had saved sufficient funds for a deposit on our current house.

Isaiah 30:21 says, "*And thine ear shall hear a word behind thee.*" *God* will guide us.

We are also told in Proverbs 3:5: "*Trust in the Lord with all of thine heart and lean not on thine own understanding*."

We read in Isaiah 55:6, "*Seek ye the Lord while he may be found. Call ye upon him while he is near.*" He will answer.

I wholeheartedly believe these scripters and tried my best to embody them, and to have them guide my going out and coming in.

"Be Strong in the Lord and in the Power of His Might." Ephesians 6:10

Be strong and of a good courage, fear not, nor be afraid of them: for the LORD thy God, he it is that doth go with thee; he will not fail thee, nor forsake thee. Deuteronomy: 31:6

But God

CHAPTER SIX

THEREFORE, I WALK IN *GOD'S* LOVE AND LIGHT.

"

Let your light so shine before men, that they may see your good works, and glorify your Father in heaven.

Matthew 5:16

I had a robust question for the Lord while I was at work and preparing to leave for the day. It was around 4 p.m. I turned to the Lord and asked, "Why are you not using my husband?" Indeed, I was hoping my husband would become a churchgoer and develop a relationship with *God* like I have. I prayed and hoped he would become actively involved in church life.

As usual, I punched my time card and went home. After dinner, I started washing dishes and getting on with my chores. That is when I heard a loud Voice say, "*I Am using him to pay the rent for you.*" Those words made me feel as though I'd gotten a slap in the face. I was puzzled and stunned. That shut me up fast.

I could no longer assume **God** was not working on my behalf. My friends, this is why we must trust **God**! We must trust Him, much like a newborn depends on the adults in their lives to feed and take care of all their needs. Let me remind you that **God** is always working in and on our lives, even when we do not see or think He is.

Throughout this book, I have been sharing my experiences as a child of **God**. I have mentioned on several occasions hearing directly from the **Spirit of God**. So I was not surprised when, one day, I was about to take some meat out of the freezer in preparation for dinner. I opened the freezer door and reached for the beef liver purchased a few days earlier. Immediately, I heard this same Voice saying, "*Do not eat that*."

Of course, in obedience, I threw the liver in the trash. I haven't eaten liver since that day. I cannot claim to understand why the *Holy Spirit* instructed me not to eat that liver. But given my past experiences and the fact that I know I am being led and directed by the *Holy Spirit,* I believe I was being protected from eating food that was no longer fresh and would ultimately lead to illness.

On another memorable occasion, one of my younger sisters invited me to Canada for a banquet that her church was organizing. At this time, my finances were not flowing the way I thought they should. I had many conversations with myself about why it was not feasible for me to attend that event. The day before the banquet, which was a Friday, I was driving to work when I heard a thundering Voice say, "*It is not your money, anyway. It's God's money*." As a result of that encounter, I immediately made the necessary arrangements and flew to Canada that night to attend the banquet.

Our Bible teaches that we are stewards of what we are blessed with. It does not belong to us.

Again, when I am hearing so clearly from the *Holy Spirit*, I know I must respond in obedience. My experience with praying and repeating scriptures came to a sudden halt one evening just before going to bed. I was sitting on the floor repeating the sixth Psalm. I said it repeatedly in a loud voice. The *Holy Spirit* then said to me, "*There is no need to*

beg God. " That was my cue. I stopped saying the sixth Psalm.

On another occasion, while I was having dinner, I heard a Voice say, '***Remember when***!" This reinforced for me that whenever I am faced with a challenge, I should remember when ***God***, in His infinite wisdom and glory, worked things out in my favor. My life and experiences show that if He did it once, He will do it again.

But God

CHAPTER SEVEN

GOD IS SPEAKING. ARE YOU LISTENING?

"

My sheep hear my voice, and I know them, and they follow me: And I give unto them eternal life; and they shall never perish, neither shall any man pluck them out of my hand.

John 10:27

I am very friendly with my neighbors who come to Florida in the winter and leave for home in Canada at the beginning of spring. One year, they left for Canada on a Wednesday and left their keys with me. I was to watch over the house as well and collect their mail.

The day after they left, their alarm went off at 1:00 am. Of course, the sheriff came and rang our doorbell. When the sheriff left, I found myself tossing and turning in bed. I could not get back to sleep. I finally fell asleep at about 4:00 am. When I woke up at 7:00 am, I was fuming. I was angry primarily because I, not my husband, had volunteered to watch over my neighbor's house and to collect their mail while they were out of the country. Yet he was the person who joined the sheriff when they arrived at my neighbor's.

My spouse was brought into the picture by default. He took over for me in this situation because of the time it occurred; he did not know what to expect.

Later that day, as I walked to my garage, I heard a loud Voice saying, "**Love your neighbor as yourself**." I then realized that my behavior was not reflective of that scripture.

As followers of Christ, we know that this is one of His commandments, to love thy neighbor as thyself. Matthew 22:39.

There is no doubt in my mind that the Voice I heard was the **Spirit of God**, correcting me for my selfish anger.

One important lesson I have learned over the years of leaning on **God** and depending on the **Holy Spirit** is the value and importance of handing our desires and needs to **God**. This realization became clearer to me when I visited a woman, Cynthia, who was a Sunday school teacher when we met.

During my visit, Cynthia told me she had to make an important decision. As a result, she got on her knees and asked **God** to intervene on her behalf. Cynthia wanted it to be the correct decision - guided by **God**. She then continued her daily activities and chores, but the challenge kept coming back to her. Cynthia then decided that she needed to start praying again.

She went back on her knees. When she finished crying out to **God** in prayer, she was at her sink as she explained to me, "I heard a Voice say to me, you already gave it to **God**. No need to take it back." Hearing that Voice had made her afraid. She checked her house from top to bottom for days to ensure no one was there.

Readers of the Bible may recall how **God** spoke to His people Psalms 32:8.

One of my most recent acquaintances is Verina. I met her at the gym some months ago. One day, after exercising, we sat on a bench, chatting. I told her I could not sit with her for too long because I had to visit the dermatologist to assess a rash on my left cheek. She replied that she, too, had an appointment for a similar rash on her face.

Verina mentioned that she heard a Voice as she stopped at the traffic light before she got to the doctor's office. It told her that her rash was caused by the laundry detergent. I knew she was a believer, and I was not in the least surprised to hear her story. At this time, I had not shared with Verina that I was contemplating writing a book about hearing the Voice of *God*.

Then there is Ms. Bartholomew, a long-time friend of mine. "I'm considering writing about hearing the Voice of *God*," I said. She gladly offered two different experiences she had.

Ms. Bartholomew grew up in Trinidad. A narrow part of the river that ran through the neighborhood she lived in as a child. She said she attempted to jump over the river one day but felt a cloud overshadow her. She heard a Voice say, "***Don't jump over that river again***." She listened.

"Then I heard the warning again," Ms. Bartholomew said. She explained to me that the narrow area was where the water flowed into a much wider part of the river. That was the first time that she had experienced the Voice.

According to her, it was the Voice of ***God*** protecting her from danger. The next time she heard the Voice of the ***Holy Spirit*** was when she lived in Brooklyn, New York. She was driving on the Gowanus Expressway when she suddenly heard a Voice say, "***Turn back***!"

Ms. Bartholomew was terrified, so she pulled over to the shoulder of the busy expressway. Suddenly, she saw a vehicle's headlights in the distance approaching her. She then realized that she was driving in the wrong direction. Thank **God** that she was obedient to the guidance of the **Holy Spirit**. If not, our paths would never have crossed. I would not be able to tell her story about the goodness of **God**.

Early in my Christian walk, I heard testimonies in churches, but I did not grasp the significance. To my naive mind, people were just airing their dirty laundry or seeking sympathy. In other words, they were sharing their business in public. I no longer feel that way. I believe that people who have been walking with **God** are commissioned to spread the good news and the glory of **God** with young Christians. If my sharing

51

has helped strengthen their faith, it has been worth my while and effort.

Even when I was dealing with a health issue. I prayed and prayed about it. The **Spirit** reminded me that **God** gets the glory when health returns.

During the process of writing this book, I have been waking up many days with this song in my spirit:

> *"Tis so sweet to trust in Jesus,*
> *just to take Him at His word.*
> *Just to rest upon His promise,*
> *Just to know, thus saith the Lord.*
> *Jesus, Jesus, how I trust Him.*
> *How I've proved Him o'er and o'er.*
> *Jesus, Jesus, precious Jesus,*
> *Oh, for grace to trust Him more."*

I am inviting anyone who reads this book or hears my story to put their trust in **God** and not to lean on their understanding. What **God** has done for and to me, He can and will do for you.

Gratitude goes to my sisters Rita and May, and my nephew Aubrey who spent countless hours assisting me to get this project together. Also, to Alia and her sister Nadia who typed my manuscript when my laptop was broken.

Finally, my friends, because my Heavenly Father provides all my needs, I can say all proceeds from this project go to charity. My **God** will supply all my needs according to His riches in glory. Philippians 4:19.

But God

ABOUT THE AUTHOR

Hazel is an American by choice who was born in Georgetown Guyana. She is a strong believer in Christ and the Word of God.

Hazel has six siblings, a husband and a grown daughter.

It is because she can confess that God is her leader and deliverer that she feels it is incumbent on her to share her testimony.

Hazel's prayer is that God will get the glory in everything that she does. That He will be seen and not her. May you be inspired by her story. You too can hear God's voice. Just draw near to Him.